THE KEY TO HAVING A SHARP MIND

Improve your mental acuity and memory recall

Sami Omar

Thank you so much purchasing this book!

If you have 60 seconds, hearing your honest feedback on this book on Amazon would mean the world to me. It does wonders for the book and I love hearing about your experience with it!

To leave your feedback please visit:

https://a.co/d/OakEr2s

or scan the QR code:

CONTENTS

INTRODUCTION
TO BOOK:

Have you accidentally locked yourself out or forgotten to turn off the stove? Or have stood dumbfounded in the doorway, unable to remember why you entered the room. We have all been there. Casual forgetfulness is a common and very human thing to experience, and it's nothing to worry about. Problems arise when you or your close ones start noticing the forgetfulness, becoming adamant and recurring.

Memory problems are more common than you'd think. But just because it is common doesn't mean that it is not frustrating. Being busy individuals that we are in our daily life, we tend to take our mental health, specifically our memory, for granted. Even a tiny or momentary lapse in our memory can hinder our busy routine.

Though, not every memory lapse can be an indicative factor of Alzheimer's or Dementia. But recurrent forgetfulness isn't good in itself, either. For busy individuals, forgetfulness can be frustrating, exhausting, embarrassing, and discouraging. But there are palatable solutions. This book has gathered all you'll need to know to try and improve your memory.

Memory is a complex psychological phenomenon and vastly different from other physiological conditions. Taking care of or improving memory requires a different and well-thought-out approach. Memory retention in the brain is a complex process. The brain itself is a complex organ too. Hence, there is no one-stop solution here; treatments and prevention remedies must be carefully curated depending on where we lag.

Memory has many categories and subcategories. Based on these divisions, each memory problem will have a different set of prescribed solutions. Each type will have a different set of keys and exercises. For instance, sensory memories require psychotherapy and restorative care. Subsequently, short-term memory problems require a variety of mental recalling as well as calculative practices. Long-term memory is the most problematic and takes the longest to heal. Countless research papers and research designs have shown that memory problems are healable.

If you've picked up this book, you know you are facing some memory issues. But the good thing is that you are familiar with and actively looking for a solution. There is no such thing as an instant fix. In other words, you can't switch on or off your memory problems. Time is required. Patience is the key. But along with that, you need good guidance. You need a source that's reliable and compact.

In the chapters following, you will get an in-depth analysis of how memory works and how anyone can tackle their memory issues for improved performance.

The first chapter will ease you into the book. It is all about the basics of memory. It also details common triggers that are sure to affect memory with long-term exposure negatively. The second chapter will tackle all the real questions. Like how practical are most home exercises? And how much sleep and diet regime can impact memory.

The third chapter surrounds the working mechanics and science of the brain. Questions like "How a human brain forms memory?" and "what are some of the main entities in the process?" will be detailed here. The fourth chapter is about the misconceptions surrounding memory. Memory is an abstract part of the mind that quickly becomes the focus of unnecessary myths. This chapter will help clarify where you should and shouldn't invest your energy and time. The fifth chapter is an essential part of this whole book. It will help you identify your problem with one of the categories of memory to see what amount of your memory requires the most work.

The sixth chapter will pick up where the fourth one left off, talking about all the scientifically proven exercises and practices that will help improve your memory.

What sets this book apart from the rest is that its concise, digestible, and presents helpful tips. Nothing in this book is sugar-coated; it's all presented in a neutral light, curated only to help you improve your memory performance genuinely.

CHAPTER 1: INTRODUCTION TO MEMORY LOSS

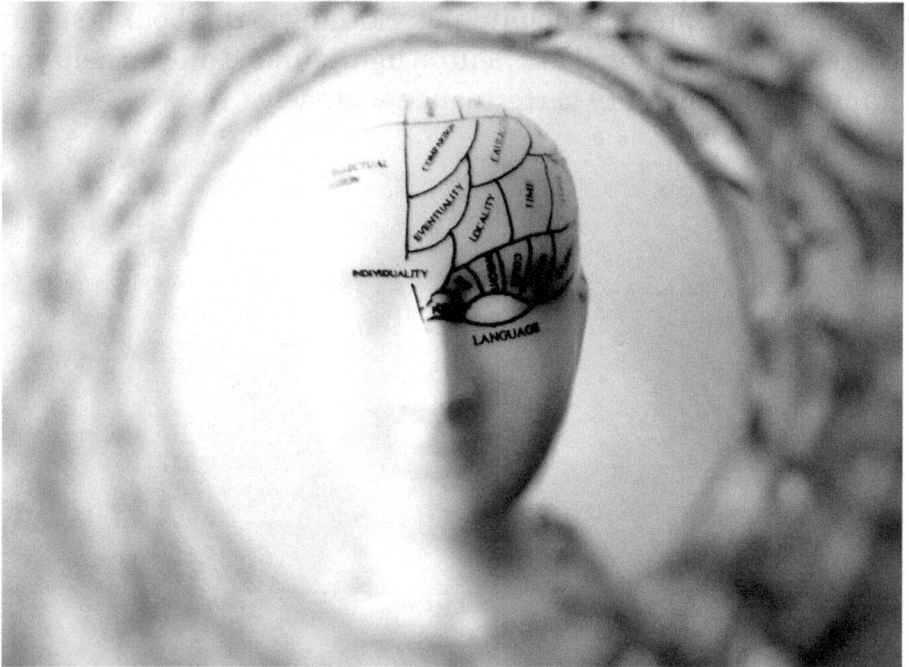

Memory storage and retention capacity have deteriorated or slowed down with age. Though unfortunate, it is pretty natural. However, compromised memory at a relatively young age is not natural. Multiple reasons may have triggered memory loss, including genetics, environment, habits, or side effects of some diseases.

Memory loss is a medical symptom of some underlying health condition, even an early indication of mental health condition. It is not to be confused with general forgetfulness. In the chapter following, a complex expression is given of what conditions fall under problematic memory loss conditions, along with a few telling vital indicators. You'll find many solutions to tackle this issue yourself in the book.

WHAT CAN BE THE TRIGGERS OF MEMORY IN ADULTS?

Though it is a breath of fresh air to see mental health conditions being talked about so openly among more prominent and global platforms, prevailing memory issues among adults everywhere are not a good sign. Memory loss is usually an indicator of some condition or persistent regimen that is taking a toll on your retention capacity.

ANXIETY:

One of the most common triggers of memory loss is anxiety. Now, it doesn't mean that anxiety causes amnesia. The term usually used is brain fog. People suffering from anxiety will usually experience blackouts during some of their episodes.

Anxiety attacks are usually coupled with a rush of cortisol and adrenaline. Both stress hormones trigger your "flight and fight" response and prepare your body for that response. Research has also concluded that high cortisol levels over a long period can lead to decreased memory retrieval ability, commonly known as "Brain fog".

DEPRESSION:

Recently, we have seen a perturbing surge in diagnosed depression cases among young adults. Depression affects more than just your mood; it affects your overall abilities, including your everyday tasks. One of the many symptoms of depression is memory loss, namely declarative memory. Declarative memory is a memory of events and incidents, casually referred to as short-term memories.

Episodic memory, however, doesn't seem to be affected by depression. This eulogy indicates that memory recovery after depression is possible to a great extent. Scientists and medical researchers have hypothesized that the onset of depression depresses the formation of new nerve cells. A lack of new nerve cells means a lack of stored memories.

PTSD:

PTSD, or Post Traumatic Stress Disorder, is another mental health condition that leads to memory retention issues. Research has shown that untreated and undiagnosed PTSD can lead to declarative memory dysfunction. PTSD can be due to any problem or experience. People who have PTSD don't share the same triggers or experiences. PTSD can be due to multiple reasons and incidents. But memory loss is a symptom seen among almost all patients with PTSD.

PTSD significantly affects a person's mental health because people who suffer from this usually try to suppress the whole incident. Prolonged suppression of undealt emotions and repression of an incident can lead to mental stress that eventually leads to memory loss.

ALCOHOLISM:

Alcoholism is a condition where excessive alcoholic beverages lead to long-term mental and physical health. Alcoholism is a health hazard and leads to numerous other detrimental effects and symptoms.

Mental and memory dysfunction is one of those things. Blacking out after drinking too much is something else. Excessive alcohol consumption can lead to brain damage. It can lead to the deterioration of nerve cells, both newly forming and old ones, putting both short and long-term memory at risk. Hippocampus is the part of the brain that deals with long-term memory retention and recall. Excessive alcohol directly affects the hippocampus.

DEFICIENCIES:

Lack of proper nutrients leads to many health conditions. Proper nutrient supplementation is a smart way to prevent almost all diseases. A healthy and balanced diet is a good start. Lack of proper supplementation can lead to more than just a few minor health conditions.

Vitamin B12 is one of the essential nutrients for a healthy body and healthy mind. Lack of vitamin B12 and old age is a perfect blend of detrimental memory dysfunction. Lower than normal vitamin B12 have been seen among patients with dementia and minimal cognitive impairment. If memory loss is due to vitamin B12, it can be remedied by taking the required supplements.

THYROID:

Subclinical thyroid is another condition that brings about many problems; memory loss is just one of them. Older patients suffering from subclinical thyroid conditions are more likely to develop dementia.

Mild thyroid conditions are not the same as subclinical thyroid. People suffering from the former are not at the same risk as the latter. Hyperthyroidism is another condition that triggers the risk of clinical memory loss. Treatment for thyroid is available now and can improve your memory.

TRANSIENCE:

Transient global amnesia is another condition that usually affects middle-aged people and seniors. As the name already suggests, it is a condition of amnesia. In this condition, amnesia comes in the form of episodes. Most patients describe these episodes as "blackouts".

There is usually a more pertaining chance of short-term memory loss, implying that many patients retain their memory along the way after a few periods.

OTHER MEDICATIONS:

Though medications are necessary for our well-being and modern sciences, they have opened many new medical achievement doors. But with antibiotic medications, some side effects. Though these side effects are presented as a little dot, effects vary from person to person and can range from light to severe.

Anti-anxiety, anti-seizure, anti-depressants, dopamine, and significant hypertension medications, to name a few, are some of the medicines with memory loss as a clear and observed side symptom. For this, a doctor's consultation may be the best solution.

CHAPTER 2: IMPORTANCE OF MEMORY AND MEMORY FACTS

The human body is very complicated. Every human process is as intricate as the next. Memory formation, storage, and retrieval are biological and chemical at the back. A proper diet and good routine can push forth or even push back these processes and pathways.

The formation of memory is an intricate process, but the human body, being a scientific marvel as it is, handles these procedures with grace, delicacy, and precision. Nerve cells are the storage houses of memories. They hold a lifetime of our memories. Just like that, the process of nerve cells is natural. Changes in the neurons in the neural activity pattern are what convert stimulations, visuals, and auditory cues into memories. Neural pattern activity helps to build a pattern so that memory retrieval is possible by following the same pattern.

More on the science behind memory later; in this chapter, you'll learn the factors that can negatively affect your memory and the types of memories most at risk with disrupted routines.

HOW MUCH YOUR MEMORY CAN IMPROVE NATURALLY?

Human body systems are very much self-sustained. A lot of the time, the human body goes through processes and responses to protect itself. But we don't even know it because those are non-conscious procedures.

This self-reliance and self-healing nature of the human body can also readily degrade with an abrupt and unhealthy lifestyle. On the other hand, it can also improve with simple life changes. Following are some factors that directly affect memory, and you can improve your mental health.

WHAT ARE SOME OF THE HABITS TO CHOOSE?

Habits can make or break you. A healthy body yields a healthy mind, and a healthy body comes from healthy habits. Following are some of the best habits to add to your routine for a more prosperous and healthy mind.

ACTIVE LIFESTYLE:

Lazing around most of the day with no actual exercise or activity routine can and will affect your mental health and, subsequently, your memory. An office job or any job requiring you to sit all day contributes to a stagnant lifestyle. Unlike a tired body, Resting cannot rejuvenate an exhausted mind via just resting. It requires more.

Keeping your body active via exercise is crucial to a healthy lifestyle, no matter how short a session is. You don't have to join a gym for this. An at-home session or a jog around the neighbourhood works just as fine. All you need is 2 hours of an aerobic routine.

Keeping your mind active is just as crucial. Falling into the same routine-like pattern can and will dull your brain. It would help if you kept it stimulated via mental exercises. Crossword puzzles, regular puzzles, and learning a new language or instrument are some mind teasers to help keep your mind alert.

SLEEP:

Disrupted sleep, not sleeping at night, not taking naps, and being unable to sleep are four very different patterns. But, all of them ultimately lead to a disturbed mind and eventually a bad memory. Sleep plays a vital role in memory.

As students, one of the best pieces of advice you can get is never to compromise your 8-hour sleep. A well-rested mind has way better recalling ability than an all-nighter mind. Do not make "pulling an all-nighter" a habit of yours. Because even though the human body is known to be adoptive, a destructive sleep cycle is something a human body will never be able to adapt to as it doesn't fulfil the required need. An 8-hour sleep is a must.

DIET:

You are what you eat. In this case, what you eat decides how your recalling power will be affected. A balanced diet doesn't necessarily mean salads and supplements. A balanced diet can include everything. Add fruits, vegetables, whole grains, low-fat proteins, and beans to your diet. And this can't be stressed enough, drink lots and lots of water. Hydration is essential for everything: your skin, body, and mind. Not drinking enough water will dry you inside out, affecting your looks and mood.

SOCIALIZING:

Socializing is one such factor that doesn't get talked about enough. Whether you are an introvert or an extrovert, socializing is essential. As human beings, we are social animals. It is in our nature to seek human contact. And this contact helps us ward off depression and a sense of loneliness which, in fact, directly affects memory recollection.

Though any degree of forgetfulness can be treated via home remedies and lifestyle changes upkeep, it is essential to know when to seek medical help. In case forgetfulness starts coming out in the form of physical impulses, that's when it is best to go to a doctor.

WHAT ARE SOME OF THE HABITS YOU HAVE TO DROP?

Habits are what we choose to do on an everyday basis. It is essential to know that. No habits are out of our control. We can omit habits just as we can add them. Not necessarily an easy task, but perfectly doable.

Alcohol intake is a proven habit that damages many organs, including the mind.

Smoking is another one. Long-term smoking habits affect the cortex directly. The cortex in your brain is what processes your memories and emotions. Studies have shown excessive smoking leads to a thinned-out cortex, affecting memory, consciousness, and emotions.

Excessive screen time also impacts memory. Research has shown that excessive screen time affects the grey and white matter in the brain. This change in the brain leads to poor concentration and degraded memory and also contributes to the onset of dementia early on.

TAKE TIME TO YOURSELF:

Taking time for yourself is a crucial part of self-discovery. On the road to self-love, it is being okay with spending time with yourself. Finding some alone time can get pretty hard with jobs, studies, family duties, and stuff. But that's what you must manage. Your mental state comes first, above all else. That's the only way you'll be able to carry on with the ups and downs of life.

When you do manage to make time, make sure to do something productive. Don't stick to your phone. Do something that will soothe your mind. Organize your closet, journal a bit, draw something or colour something, dance around, and read a book. Unwinding yourself at the end of the day is just as important as starting your day with good energy and high spirits.

CHAPTER 3: DISCOVERING THE BRAIN

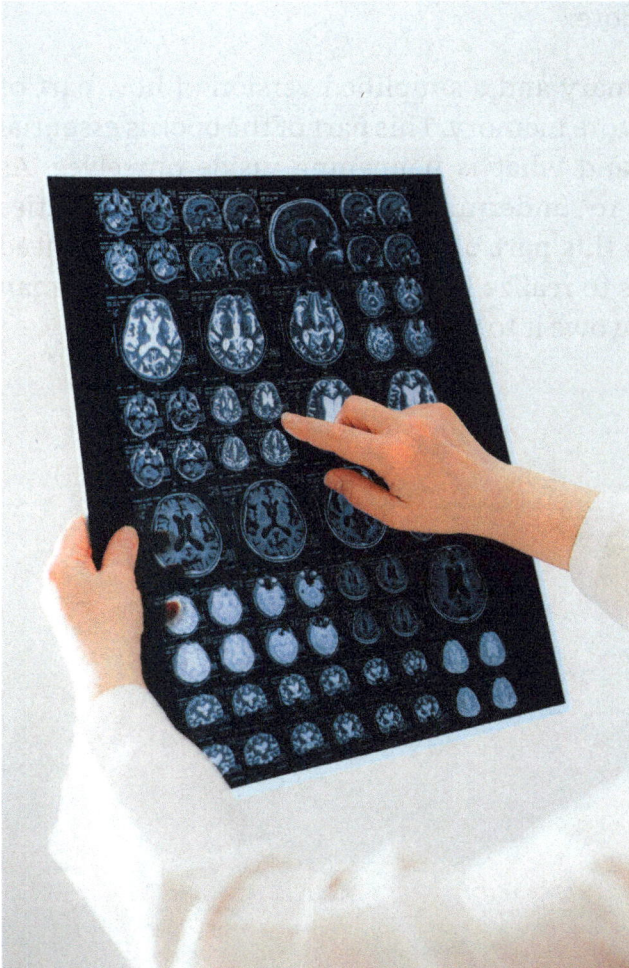

The human brain is a complex organ. There are lots of neurotransmitter connections that are wiring, rewiring, and disconnecting at the same time. These connections help us flow our thoughts and emotions throughout our life. The human brain has parts, and each part has a related function.

All brain parts come together to work synergistically to elicit a response. Thousands upon thousands of neurons in your brain are working together so that you can remember things. Next time you feel stupid, remind yourself that millions of cells in your body and brain are working tirelessly to help you sustain through life. And that is worth a lot more.

Following is a summary and a simplified version of how part of our brain works to store memory. This part of the book is essential to help us understand what is happening inside ourselves. As humans, we tend to undermine ourselves and our abilities constantly. Though this part of the book is scientific, you need to read through this to realize how much of a marvel the human brain is and how you owe it to take care of yourself.

THE MEMORY CHURNER IN THE BRAIN:

Throughout the years, Scientists and researchers have thought that only a segment of the human brain is responsible for storing memories like a separate folder in a drawer. Karl Lashley was the first ever scientist to hypothesize this. He called it the "Engram". Though his findings didn't support his hypothesis, he discovered that it isn't one part of the brain responsible for memories; it's a lot.

AMYGDALA:

Let's go back a few hundred centuries. Humans evolved to have memories and recollections as a survival tactic. Cave dwellers had to remember routes, good foods, poisonous food, and experience to live through. Amygdala regulates what we know as negatively aggressive emotions, such as fear and aggression. These emotions are essential for memory storage, as much of memory storage relies on stress hormones.

On top of that, the amygdala also hoists memories from short-term folders to long-term storage when the memory is triggered by fear, anger, or emotional distress. The Pavlovian conditioning analysis also showed that the conditioned memory was stored and projected by the amygdala.

HIPPOCAMPUS:

Hippocampus is what is directly and physically related to memory storage. Research has shown that infusing lesions in the hippocampus can lead to memory impairment in mouse models. This experiment alone was enough to deduce that the hippocampus is the main working machine regarding memory storage.

Hippocampus also helps to transfer memory to the cortex. This cortex works to associate each memory with meaning and develops connections and consistencies among different memories. The hippocampus is the closest researchers have gotten to depicting the role of the engram, proving to be the primary source of processing senses into memories.

CEREBELLUM:

Though the hippocampus is the processing unit of memories, the cerebellum is where these memories are used. These memories are turned into learning incidents, i-e. These incidents are noted in the long-term memory and put to use practically to alter a response. One such experiment allowed the rabbits to learn to blink upon a trigger. A disrupted cerebellum of the rabbit caused them to forget the conditioned blinking response.

The cerebellum is the part of the brain that allows you to learn from accidents and anecdotes by simply shifting memories in the knowledge folder.

PREFRONTAL CORTEX:

The prefrontal cortex plays a significant role in memory recall. A lot of the time, one experience is enough for us to learn, while others take a few rounds. You may have noticed that a single life-threatening incident is enough for us to think about our choices and access our deep-held values in life. That's the survival feature of talking. And these features are via the cortex, which eases memory recall.

Experimental research has also shown that the inferior prefrontal cortex is the most active when recalling previously shown words. The prefrontal cortex handles the task context of learning memory. It encodes, updates, and maintains the memory of your everyday tasks and routine.

NEUROTRANSMITTERS

:

Science is still pretty developing when it comes to an understanding of the human brain. We know that there are multiple neurotransmitters, each of which may perform a separate function. But researchers still haven't been able to decode the exact function of these neurotransmitters. But we know that the neurotransmitter connection and communication are vital for developing new memories and solidifying previous ones.

WHAT HAPPENS DURING MEMORY LOSS?

There may be multiple reasons for memory loss. It may be due to amnesia, persistence, transience, misinformation, or encoding error. In the case of middle-aged adults, the most common is an encoding error. It is hard to find something in your drawer that you never put in there. That's precisely the case with encoding errors.

Memory is not stored in the brain if it is not studied and noticed thoroughly. Something you glance over once is harder to recall than what you saw and read multiple times throughout the day. That's because repeated exposure helps to sustain the memory long-term.

THE METAPHYSICS BEHIND MEMORY:

To understand the metaphysics behind memory, we need to understand the term RTM or Representational Theory of Memory. This theory suggests that the human brain does not hold a specific memory's exact, frame-by-frame recollection. Instead, the memory that we have is just a few highlight images.

A good example would be a wedding day or a graduation day. These days are considered social milestones and are usually significant days. But, even then, the human brain doesn't hold all the seconds of that day. Instead, it remembers highlights of the day, like the cake, the dress, or the first dance. There may be hints of how you felt or what emotions you went through. In short, you have a summarized memory stored of any memory that you have.

CHAPTER 4: MYTHS ABOUT MEMORY: STRENGTHENING AND WEAKENING

Whilst there is a lot already known about memory, there are still a few grey areas, areas that need more research and more understanding. As mentioned above, the human brain is super complex in how memory works and processes depend on several factors. Hence, this is why each individual gets a "customized"

treatment.

No treatment follows the narrative of "one size fits all" and not the brain and, subsequently, the memories. For social convenience, we tend to group all memory issues into one. Forgetfulness is not the same as dementia. If you forget your car keys one day, this doesn't mean you are developing Alzheimer's. Similarly, forgetting the entire map of the house you've lived in for years isn't silly absentmindedness.

In short, one solution can not fit all. You may have heard many things that positively or negatively affect your memory. Some may sound genuine; some may sound questionable. The following chapter is all about busting these myths.

A SECRET RECIPE:

Companies and sometimes people tend to advertise random habits, activities or food-based, such as an instant cure, a miracle solution or a secret recipe. As much as we all would like to believe that, it just isn't the case. We are complex beings with even more complex working machinery inside. Nothing can work as a switch on or off button. Whether it is gaining health or losing health, both are gradual processes.

To preserve memory and strengthen your mind, you need to work and keep at it. Changing your diet, sleep schedule, daily routine, and workout regime would be best. Everything!

You'll also not see results in a day, a week or even a month. But you will see it gradually changing and shifting over time. Heck, even supplements take time longer than a few weeks. Keep working; keep at it. You'll see the gradual positive change.

EDIBLES ARE THE ONLY WAY:

Relying on edibles is a cultural approach. In many cultures, it is believed that the stomach route can solve all diseases and problems. This eulogy is accurate in a lot of cases. Diet, home remedies, and oral medications can improve your overall well-being. However, this is not true in all cases.

General forgetfulness triggered by a poor diet or stressed routine can be remedied using nuts and fatty fish, but they can't go so long. You have to include other activities and alterations in your life.

Along with edibles, supplements and healthy food and all, you have to opt for healthy activities. Exercise your mind and your brain. Keep both stimulated and active for healthy existence. Research has shown that people with a healthy and active lifestyle are less likely to have age-induced memory issues.

AGE FACTOR LIMITATION:

Being too old or too young to change is also a social construct that is sometimes used in spaces that aren't age-restricted. Like how no one is too old or too young to like cartoons. But people may be too old or young to jump bungees due to health hazards. But memory building is not such a thing.

Working on strengthening your memory isn't something that is age dependent. It isn't like skincare. You can start working on improving your memory at any age. The younger generation can yield good benefits from improving their memory, which will help them with their studies—as for seniors, improving your memory will impose several positive impressions on your overall health.

MIND CLUTTERING:

Mind cluttering is another relative factor that can trigger memory loss. Previous research has deduced that memory deterioration with age is usually due to mind cluttering, as senior citizens tend to have more memories than younger subjects.

Research has also shown that senior citizens tend to hold on to information, no matter how random it may be, causing an overload of information. This overload of excess information is what clutters our minds. Similar to trying to find a t-shirt in a giant walk-in closet.

Screen time is one such prevalent example of factors inducing mind cluttering. Smartphones are dubbed as having "the whole world in your hand", which is figuratively true. With smartphones, you can google anything. But, with smartphones and social media, you get a hefty daily dose of random and irrelevant-to-you information, thus cluttering your mind and dragging down your memory strength.

MUSCLE-LIKE EXERCISE REGIMEN:

There is a misconception that the mind, like any other organ, can be exercised. Yes, the brain is an organ that needs stimulation and exercise. But not like how you'd exercise your biceps. Our brain is a little too complicated for its sound. Our brain receives many signals and responds based on those signals. Each response is curated, catering to that stimulus. Doing puzzles cannot help your memory altogether.

There are different types of memory. Each memory has different triggers and different stimuli. Doing puzzles will make you good at puzzles, but it won't improve your memory retaining power. Hence, doing various exercises to stimulate most of your brain would be best. There is no one-way solution.

A SHORTCUT:

There is no shortcut, I repeat, no shortcut when it comes to memory and mind. The mind requires patience and diligence. You can't expect your memory to improve drastically with one supplement dose. Expecting to see noticeable results within weeks is also a bit of reach. It'll take time.

It's not just the memory building that'll take time; all the activities you'd have to include to improve your memory will also take time. Though the human body is adapted to change, it can't do so linearly. The physical exercise, the diet improvement, the sleep schedule rescheduling, the supplements and the little habits you'd have to leave. It will take time, and it's okay. The human body takes time, and that's normal. Remember to be persistent, but also be kind to yourself throughout the process. A positive mindset throughout is essential here.

CHAPTER 5: MEMORY TESTING

Testing your memory is a critical step in knowing where you stand. Often than not, self-diagnosis via the help of the internet is misleading and inaccurate. You end up either overcompensating or under compensating your condition. These memory tests are not designed to help you diagnose yourself; they help you know where you stand.

Types Of Memory:

You see, memory isn't just one entity. There are many different types of memory. There is episodic memory, semantic memory, implicit memory, explicit memory, echoic memory and autobiographical memory. Let's take a look at each of these types.

Episodic memory is declarative memory that holds all your personal and first-hand experiences. These memories are the most vivid as they are translations of incidents that you have experienced. Episodic memory is bound to deteriorate with age and neurodegenerative disorders.

Retrograde and anterograde amnesia are two disorders that occur when episodic memories are compromised. Retrograde amnesia is an inability of the brain to form new episodic memory. This amnesiac condition occurs with the onset of ageing as older people cannot recall what they did last year but can easily recall incidents that happened in their teens.

Subsequently, anterograde memory is the inability to recall what happened at one point. This amnesiac condition is usually triggered by trauma.

Semantic memory is the part of memory that holds all of our general knowledge, like names and phone numbers, and vocabulary. Deterioration of semantic memory is seen among Alzheimer's patients.

Implicit memory holds all such memories you do not consider much: the background memories. These are your internalized and long-term memories that are subconscious and key factors. They affect your mood and behaviour in your everyday life. Implicit memory damage is very clearly seen among Alzheimer's patients. There is still a lot yet to be known about implicit memory.

Explicit memory is a retrospective of implicit memory. Explicit memory is all the information, concepts and experiences that you consciously and "explicitly" add to your memory, like remembering to get your oil changed on the first Saturday of every month. But, these memories are bound to be forgotten once they are out of your daily routine. For instance, if you haven't driven your car in a year, you'd have forgotten about the monthly oil changes.

As the name already hints, **Echoic memory** is sensory memory formed from auditory stimuli. The most common example would be the lyrics of a song you heard ages ago. Echoic memories are somewhere between long-term and short-term memories. Some auditory memories can last quite a period, while others aren't as long-lasting. Infants and toddlers have susceptible auditory memory as they pick up on words, tones and sounds they hear from their surroundings.

Autobiographical memory is an amalgam of semantic and episodic memory. It's a collection of the most important or memorable events and experiences of one's life. The most vivid effects of autobiographical memory can be seen among schizophrenia patients suffering from mild cognitive impairment.

TYPES OF MEMORY TESTS:

EYEWITNESS TEST:

The eyewitness test is a simple and fun psychological test. These tests are usually in the form of visual motion signals and stimulants set to check how much you can recall from what you have seen in the last period. What sets eyewitness tests apart from tray tests in motion? In the eye witness test, you see things move, like how they'd be in normal bustling circumstances.

Being able to differentiate crucial memory from irrelevant one in a crowded environment is an example of exceptional episodic memory. Visual or episodic memory is the strongest and is admissible in conviction court as well.

MEMORY RECOLLECTION TEST:

The memory recollection test, or MRT, is another simple and fun psychological test. Quite similar to the eyewitness test but differs only in the stimuli. The eyewitness test heavily relies on what we see in an environment. The memory recollection test relies on word recalling rather than an item.

There are many memory tests online that you can take to see how well you can recall. This test is also an exercise that is recommended for people suffering from the early onset of Alzheimer's.

TRAY TEST:

A tray test is a great way to test your short-term memory to see how much information you can retain in a short period.

How it works is that a volunteering individual is presented with a tray covered with a towel. This tray has a collection of somewhat random items. The towel is removed, and each volunteer is shown the items on the tray for a short time. Afterwards, each individual is asked to list all the objects they can remember from the tray.

WHAT'S MISSING TEST:

What's missing test judges how well you can connect one memory to the other. What's a missing test not only checks your short-term memory but does so independent of your retrieval power. You see, memory retention and memory retrieval are two separate phenomena. Most of the time, these two are used synonymously.

It works that each participating individual is presented with a bunch of random digits. Each participant is allowed to study the numbers. Afterwards, one or more of these numbers are removed. Each participant is then asked to tell which number is missing.

THE CALCULATION TEST:

While most other tests were simply based on what you say, the calculation test takes it further. The test doesn't only consider your retaining and recalling qualities but also your calculation and analytical abilities.

Each individual is shown a bunch of random digits in this memory test. After some time, each individual is asked to recall those numbers. Afterwards, the calculation test starts. Each participant is then asked to multiply some numbers with the list of numbers recalled earlier. This portion judges your multitasking skills.

So, you're well informed about the aspects involved with your memory. Now, it's time to end the book with valuable exercises to enhance your memory. Let's move further and get surprised.

CHAPTER 6: EXERCISES TO BOOST MEMORY AMONG ADULTS

Practice makes a man perfect. If you want to perfect a skill, you should work long and hard for it. Memory boosting is no different. Boosting memory requires just as much work as any other skill. Now, to define "work," there are several factors. One of the most decisive factors is mind teasers and exercises.

Many of these mind teasers and mind exercises deemed the best isn't for everyone. Puzzles are one of the exercises that are encouraged in almost every article you'll find online. But puzzles have a lesser tendency to help improve memory. No research can help to improve your memory. Yes, it activates and stimulates your mind, but it won't help your overall memory health.

SCIENTIFICALLY PROVEN EXERCISES:

Here, we have a few scientifically proven exercises that will help you stimulate your mind to the point it can improve your memory. You'll see vivid results with regular practice.

MNEMONICS:

Mnemonics are learning techniques that are readily seen being used in schools to help students retrieve information efficiently. Mnemonic devices are a set of practices that allow you to remember information better. The most common example would be the alphabet song. No matter how old, we still remember our ABCs because we learned them with a delightful tune. Another example would be remembering the number of days each month via knuckles.

You can use rhymes, tunes, and even imaginary libraries to retain as much memory as possible while maintaining good retrieval ability. Another helpful tip would be doodling. Doodling ideas and mind maps can help you retrieve memory better than muddled-up words.

ORGANIZING INFORMATION:

Information needs to be organized to be revisited and retrieved easily. Categorizing and dividing the information into bite sizes will help it stay in memory for longer.

The chunking method is the most useful method for high schoolers and university students. Chunking methods state that to learn better, try to highlight the important physical and mental texts. The highlighted text will then be easier to store in memory.

ASSOCIATIVE TECHNIQUE:

The Association technique is a memorizing technique that people already use daily. As the name implies, the association technique means associating newly introduced information with the information already on our minds. If someone's last name, some store's name, or something on the menu made you chuckle, then you are more likely to remember that than a basic name.

Similarly, a piece of new information that you can relate to some other information will stay in your memory for longer. You can use this technique in your everyday life too.

LEARNER TYPES:

Learning what type of learner you are is very important. Being categorized this way will help you understand what kind of approach will suit you the best when it comes to memory. For students, it is best to identify themselves with one of the types to cater to their memory.

Visual learners can retain certain pieces of information best when they see them. For instance, visual learners learn best with animations and drawings rather than written or spoken words.

Auditory learners can store information the best when they have heard it. Classroom settings are best for auditory learners. If you are an auditory learner, try to say things out loud to remember them better.

Kinesthetic learners learn the best when they do something, a.k.a; people who remember the best from their experience. This learner should do or imagine themselves in certain settings to help retain those experiences in their memory.

Reading/Writing learners learn the best with a reading and writing regime. Some learners need just to read some text to memorize it. Some need to write it down to remember things better. Some require both, writing the piece of information down after reading about it. These types of learners tend to be most organized.

RECALL AND REHEARSAL:

Random recalling is an important part of memory exercise. Test yourself constantly and randomly to see how well you can recall. It doesn't have to be a critical piece of information; you can set any random words for yourself to remember and then place those words to see how well you remember. You can do this exercise anytime and anywhere.

As for rehearsal, it is essential to ensure good memorization. Repetition is one of the best tricks to learn something faster and for longer. A lot of people are unable to retain much different unrelated information as it clutters the mind, like a grocery list. But, if you stick the grocery list on your fridge and see it many times every day, you'll eventually remember it.

BUILDING ROUTINES AND CHARTS:

As mentioned above, you must stay organized. Track your progress and routine. Check your way to see the best time to add new mind exercises to your practice. Analyze your regime to see at what time of the day you are available and at what time you are the busiest. Add mind exercises to both of those times. This organized regime will help you see how your memory is affected under calm and stressed conditions. Subsequently, use charts and lists to visualize your progress and know where you need more help.

Surround yourself with positive people who'd encourage you throughout the process. A positive support system is shown to motivate people and encourage them to keep working on themselves to improve.

APPRECIATE YOURSELF:

Tracking your progress will help you not only to monitor where you lack but will also help you to appreciate all the efforts you have put in. Positive reinforcement and mindset are keys to better health, body, and mind.

Appreciating yourself is a form of self-love and self-validation. Both of these things will help you boost your confidence. Push yourself to work hard, enjoy your effort, rejoice with the results and stay motivated to keep the results.

BOOK CONCLUSION

Well, you made it to the end. Good for you. Now, you have all the information you need to make necessary changes in your life and, ultimately, strengthen your memory. Patience is the key. You must make consistent and steady daily changes to ensure positive results.

Before finishing the book, let's briefly review all the chapters discussed.

Memory problems are relatively common, and that's because of multiple factors and triggers—our daily habits such as terrible sleep routine, lousy diet, and excessive alcohol consumption.

Mental disorders directly affect your memory. Our habits are what make and break us, so improved memory heavily relies on what your routines are.
Amygdala, hippocampus, cerebellum, cortex, and nerves play a significant role in forming and storing memories.

There are multiple myths on the internet that are either misleading or downright harmful. Eating certain foods won't improve your memory overnight. Memory improvement has no shortcuts. It is a long road and will require consistency and patience.

There are a lot of exercises on the internet, but most of these exercises are best for improving episodic memory. But there are other types of memory too. There is explicit, implicit, semantic, and autobiographical memory. Problems with either will have a different set of treatments. Multiple locations of online tests are available to see which memory of yours is suffering. Eye witness, tray, and calculation tests are the most telling.

Lastly, depending on your organization and associative skills, as well as mnemonics and recollection exercises, keep your mind active and your memory at its best.

Don't forget to be kind to yourself. Most of us are very hard on ourselves. Being unkind to yourself will lead to automatic stress buildup, and this stress will then marinate and come up as memory problems. So, be gentle with yourself. We, as humans, are allowed to make mistakes. It's in our nature; to err is to be human.

The process of improving your memory is also extensive and slow. Stress-induced memory loss isn't something that shows up randomly. It incubates for a long time, insinuated by bad eating habits and unhealthy sleep cycles. The road to recovery and improvement has a lot of hurdles along the way. But, before you move ahead, you have to go back. All the habits and cyclic routines that triggered the memory loss will require assessment for extensive help.

So, from today, take a step, however small it may be, towards improving your memory and use gentle words with yourself along the process. Gather all the positive reinforcements you can get. Appreciate the small achievements and keep at them. Good luck!

Notes

Notes

Notes

Notes

Notes

Notes

NOTES

NOTES

Made in the USA
Coppell, TX
09 November 2024

39597493R00046